In the Next Life

Joan Baranow

Poetic Matrix Press
www.poeticmatrix.com

Also by Joan Baranow

Author:

Blackberry Winter
Living Apart
Morning: Three Poems

Editor:

Tell Me, Again
The Healing Art of Writing
Poets on Parnassus
80 on the 80s: A Decade's History in Verse

Contents

I

*I would brush your sprouting hair of the
dying light...*
— *Galway Kinnell*

Believing   11
Remember These Things   12
Light Climber   13
What They Say   14
At Eye Level   15
Big History   16
From This Distance   17
Pet Cat   20
Grass Seeds   21
Global Weirding   22
Ode to *QI*   24
Rescuing Brown Marmorated Stink Bugs   26
Dear Future   28
10th Grade Science   30
Some Advice for Being Here   32
En Route   33

II

*You can't have it back, says the fire
affectionately. You never needed it
anyway, promises the earth.*
— *Dean Young*

Psalm   37
Thanksgiving Dinner   38
Gathering Asphodel   39
For My Mother   40
By Now   45
Ode to Keats   46
Emptying   47
Prescription   48

Duty Call   50
Goldilocks   51
Finding Him   53
Last Days   55
At This Hour   57
Hospital Museum   58

III

Thou, silent form, dost tease us out of thought
As doth eternity: Cold Pastoral!

— *John Keats*

Postcard   61
Cold Pastoral   62
Dear Odysseus   64
Vagabond   66
Eros   68
Imaginary Lover   70
Looking Ahead   72
Ars Poetica   75
In the Next Life   78
Ode to That   80
All That You See   82
Blue   83
Anthology: a collection of flowers   84
Moon   87

Notes

Acknowledgments

Author Biography

For David, who's always ready
to read another poem

In the Next Life

I

I would brush your sprouting hair of the dying light . . .

— Galway Kinnell

Believing

I believe in wrapping the baby in the blanket.
I believe in the father jingling his keys.

I believe in forgiving the son who dented the car,
the daughter who lost her new shoes.

I believe in recess at school, reasonable roads,
neighbors who sleep late on Saturdays,
who lend you eggs for the cake.

I believe in sharing the cake.

I believe in symphonies and rock concerts.
Otherwise, small groups will do —
poetry readings and the like.

I believe in nature's wallop, floodwaters,
wild lilies, the slipperiness of minutes,
the usual moon and tides.

I believe, too, in the mania of the many —
countries counting munitions,
subtracting soldiers from the list.

I believe nothing will change this.
Not prayer, nor uniformed officers.

Peace and terror forever,
like the heart's swell and cramp,
like our wish to rescue the vanishing wolves.

Remember These Things
— for Duston

by which the world works: the earth twirling
like that striped ball you've just tossed
for the first time overhand to me.
Nor does the sun burn, truly, but translates
matter into energy. Remember the split atom,
the sound your cereal makes exploding in milk.
I would explain batteries, magnets, radio
waves flowing positive to negative,
how anything that moves
makes a sound. There is so much
I fail to understand. You will know what to do.
You lean against glass windows, fearless.
You put whatever you like into your mouth.
Already you believe power is water,
splashing your bath into foam.
You know that flowers bloom because they like you.
Soon you will learn how the world
can snap a bone, bring a bird to the ground.
If disaster cripples you,
remember these years of easy rightness,
when I kissed your bloody scrapes.
Remember inventions, the first
microscope and toaster, hairdryer
and the horseless carriage, how we gazed
together at this book of beginnings.

Light Climber

A tree, naturally. And concrete steps,
rails, curbs, chain link,
cement risers that run along stairs.

He lifts against gravity,
muscles full of flight.
How does light climb the tree?

As you do, swinging
its own weight up, though
what do I know about light,

except through you
rising branch by branch,
beyond worry and warning,

as carefree as the dead,
who can't hear us
when we call.

What They Say

They say the universe isn't slowing down
but speeding up. Ice crystals
beyond Pluto whirl away
towards other suns. My friend
turns too fast on her bicycle,
feels her wheels flip up and she flies
down to gravel on her elbow.
Gravity's hard work, gravity's lack of humor.
Our own sun, chubby and sweaty,
our burning Buddha, pulls us
with invisible strings, though
someday we will find the one
equation that balances weightless
thoughts against stardust.
How difficult it is some evenings
just to climb the stairs.
"It's a matter of entropy," they say.
"Move faster."

At Eye Level

Gnats like being eye to eye,
unlike bees and flies and,
well, most creatures.

On a bench you'll be surprised
by a passing squirrel's
dropped seeds, half an acorn

gnawed through the middle.
A fly might light on
an open book,

but he's otherwise occupied.
Those frogs along the water's rim,
one looking that way,

one another, rest there
like old men
(minus arthritis).

And fish! What do they see
of trees and sky
but a world without edges, reflective,

like looking into a spoon
at your own
estranged features?

Big History

They're measuring the age of the earth
by what it's lost — isotopes
leaching like childhood,
leaving you with a faulty memory
and rheumatoid arthritis.
Earth, is that how you feel?
How bad does an earthquake hurt?
We've been trampling you for years,
losing our hair, our senses,
all the while growing
a cortex that invents
new ways to strangle you.
We're like strangers in a bar
sizing each other up
until one throws a punch —
sometimes it's a thousand mile pipe line,
sometimes a tornado.
Afterward, the humans stand around
to gaze at torn lumber, a broken jaw.
It must be a law that came
with the Big Bang,
one no one saw coming.

From This Distance

An ant clambers onto my sandal,
strikes out across my toe,
is joined by others like water

sucked through a straw.
Is it awe I want to feel?
Am I supposed to know

about these furry-edged leaves
whose berries are bluing?
To my left an aspen snapped

at the waist. Several here
have avalanched
as if with sappy brains

they've judged their own heft
and heaved over. We can't be everywhere
though to touch a particle

alone in space
jars another. Even an eight-year-old
can see the empty swing

sway. But this is simple.
Explain instead the moth's physics,
its unsteady flight

dipping and doubling
back with blind, frenetic tack
though it sees

with fifty more eyes
than ours. What am I asking?
The sun grows the shadows,

I'm tired of the strict music in my head,
"the wind's entreaties,"
which are not the wind's

but my own grief
gasping its speech, poetry's
hypnosis.

Distrust. Distrust.
Pick the bee's legs of their pollen.
Thrust your hand down

a snake's throat. Wheel yourself
into the operating room.
Watch how lovingly they scrape

the bodies out. Cough up
something sick. Is this it?
What? Have we finished

gnawing our bones?
Have I?
An ant is dragging

a dead larva
three times its size towards me.
I know you know that

but I won't stop the words.
They are beating out the – O –
briefest pilot light. Inferno.

NYC Sept 11, 2001 / Olympic Valley, CA

Pet Cat

What's left: a few tablespoons
of dust – flaky, granular, chips
inside a cheap box.
You must know I opened it
reluctantly when you asked.
I'd never seen the ash
of a beloved before, outside
the Society of the Humane.
I unclasped the clip
to find this paltry handful,
grit you might have scooped
from the sidewalk.
Why did they turn him into dust?
Ashes to ashes, only we're not
just that. It was weeks later
I figured out your fear.
Honey, sweetheart, he died first,
then they made him into dust.
Forgive me, I'm learning
so little as I go.
The box sits atop a chest
behind a clutter of CDs
cameras and extension cords.
When we're ready we'll bury him
beside our other cat
(who died whole at home)
on the hill under the rhododendrons.

Grass Seeds

Like tiny peacock tails
or the quick upturn of a duck's tuft.

Blanched stalks
that latch to your socks.

A greenish one holds to its seeds
like a thin spinster
while another sends out long needles topped
with Japanese-style fans —
small hands stuck on a wiry wrist.

A done daisy, hay frond, a hairy poof like a mare's tail.

A lavender cluster without the flowers,
how any could serve to make a delicate mark.

One spiraled with pale mustard blossoms
leaves a pollen imprint on the page.

Another's random branches has symmetrical leaves
no larger than a lizard's tongue.

The tape itself, torn by a strong thumb,
makes sure these spears won't drift away.
Arrayed on the glass-topped coffee table,
a meadow in miniature, like wallpaper.

Global Weirding

— a diversion, and now the stream bed
grows hot, reveals its trash: the usual
beer glass, book jacket, coil
of rusted rebar erupting from concrete
a bulldozer toppled over.
From here to waterfall it's all

stones like a nest of dusty eggs.
A few asters crowd the upper lip
of the bank, but otherwise
steel I-beams rise in predictable symmetry.
The roofline is busy before the first snow.
You can watch well-dressed workers

whisk water away from the hotel.
A veneer of piped music helps
smother raw materials.
Wolf whistle. *Hey, baby.*
What, exactly, he said, doesn't matter.
He was enjoying the old ways

when they put unwanted relatives
beyond the pale.
Also lepers, bastards, distasteful
jokes, and painted ladies
who nonetheless crept back in
under subtler guises. Injustice

prefers soft-nosed rabbits.
Cruelty, ants. On Friday nights
they are learning to ballroom dance.
Late guests include liberals
who fox-trot for prosperous deaths.
Their fingerprints end up on

fundamentalists' empties.
Let's be pastoral. Let's watch the avalanche on TV.
For a few bucks, the sign says,
you can scavenge mementos: a ski pole,
a logoed cap. Scrap of shoe buckle.
You know by the tears how well-meant we are.

Come spring there'll be new invitations.
After the fines are paid, the sign says,
you can walk on the watered grass.

Ode to *QI*

Does sound weigh more than light?
What's the golden-handed tamarin?
"Poetry's a good provider of the strange"
but has nothing on the orb-web spider
that pulls off his own penis to run faster
after her, 100 times his size.
Good thing he's got a spare pedipalp,
but as you guessed
she'll eat him afterwards for breakfast.
Or the lamppost-long
bowhead whale's mouth "cock"
thrust out like that to cool the brain,
or so they say, they say half the facts
today will be disproven by the future,
even easy stuff we made up
can't be explained:
Why passenger and not passager?
Messenger, not messager?
Words are weird like that,
a river bouncing off our tongues
half spit, part music
made of muscle, blown by breath.
What's up between a cough and *cough*?
This morning I nuked some tea,
pondered disconnection's oblivion,
RSVP'd an invite from my friends.
The ear alone's our dictator, no wonder
students hate their grammar.
So where's this poem going? O! *QI*

accept this missive as my thanks
for info so delightful and obscure.
For what it's worth, here's a puzzle:
Where does ice as thin as window panes
heave stones across a desert?

Rescuing Brown Marmorated Stink Bugs

You know those apple dimples? That's where
they stick their proboscis in and suck
teaspoons of juice.

It takes an evolved tongue, not like
shoving a straw into a watermelon.

When we tire of gin and tonic,
tears will do.

You thought the heat had passed but
today's sun bristles the skin.
Still, she's out there riding the mower,
snapping grass in half,
making a bouquet of diesel and chlorophyll.

What's the upshot of the dream
where your son flung himself off
the 10-storey foam-filled vinyl slide?

A stream below, boulders, a piney woods.

He drops. You watch.
Words cling to your mouth.
just as, about to, gimme a minute —

When you wake, the clanging stops.

This stink bug, flecked with iridescence,
steps from the plastic cup
onto the porch rail,

tips, tips over, tips back,
splits its wings. Flies.

In fact, we prefer tears,
tasting, as they do, of the womb.

Dear Future

Preliminary treatment uses screens or grinders to capture or macerate solids such as wood, Q-tips, and dead alligators so they don't muck up the works further down the line.

— Dave Praeger

We tried, really. When ooze gooped up the ocean
we invented suction to separate plastic from salt
but too many dolphins got torn apart in the process
and you know how we feel about dolphins.
After that Congress canceled the Internet
and put the country in reverse.
No one could remember bologna sandwiches
or *Simon Says* anymore anyway.
The Super Bowl, however, remained
high octane. We hosted parking lot brawls
and instantaneous T-shirts.
Not so Women's Lib weeping at the seams.
It all depends on what we thought was real.
Sidewalk cracks were avoided.
As were robo-calls. Even the thought
of lab animals patched up for the night.
We could never agree on which death
was best for the country. On whose terms.
Humans had become immune to irony.
We engineered nets to catch the suicides,
then legislated assisting them to death.
Please know these were the good days
before you replaced us. We thought
nothing of trading hearts among species,
injecting toxins to effect a cure, passing
the body through enormous magnets to map

the damaged gut.
It was good times. It was plenty
of packaged beef, bubble wrap, clam shell,
call waiting, deodorant, non-stop flights,
zero prime rate, Safe Zone training, and
antimicrobial copper-alloy surfaces
too slick to stick to, though
measles made a late comeback at Disneyland.
It was easy to get sweet on nature
with a bottle of amoxicillin in the fridge.
We stripped off lead paint and installed seat belts.
We figured death happened to other people
for the best reasons. The worst, they say,
was picking Q-tips by hand out of
sewer grates. That was 10% of the job.
The rest was shoveling sludge from city drains.
As I said, despite being a bickering, tormented lot,
we tried. We really did.

10th Grade Science

My son's assignment is to make
a model of DNA:
cytosine, thiamine, guanine, adenine
(as he reminds me).
I picture dowel sticks,
ping pong balls, hangers
bent at awkward angles,
screws and glue.
Yet how to capture
deoxyribonucleic acid's
frantic action,
a sinuous ax, splitting
while doubling,
as in the swish of Disney's
sorcerer's broom?
O – impatient cells!
O – undeterred division!
Helpless and intent,
you make leaf mold,
lunar moth, psoriasis,
bone, blood, apple blight
and puckered lips.
You are the main ingredient,
our comfort food, angel cake,
meat of the nut,
pungent blastocyst,
whole wheat yeasty

science experiment,
our baking soda and vinegar volcano,
or — on other days —
Mentos and Diet Pepsi.

Some Advice for Being Here
— for Gabriel

Never leave home without binoculars.
You won't want to miss the blue hair-streak,
jet streams, or the silhouette at dusk
who goes *teep teep teep*
chee-chee-chee-chee-chee!
Bring its name back home to put inside
your father's felt-lined cigar box.
Remember never to say "killer fudge"
in your brother's presence (you know
how sensitive he is). You may grow taller
than he but please refrain from
lifting him up to prove it.
Fake wrestling is okay. Fake biting
can cause unintentional injury.
Each morning may you open your eyes
to oaks that have survived the ambrosia beetle.
May you roller blade. May you swim
with dolphins who recognize in your bulbous forehead
one of their own sweet-natured beings.
May your gray eyes mollify nervous bullies.
May you build things that last:
vases stuck with shellacked shells,
chainsaw grizzly bears, a pigeon coop.
Whatever you make I will want
to feel its plastic hide, admire its wood grain.
I know you'll tire of my late night phone calls.
I'll keep your number on a crumpled post-it
in my pocket just to read from time to time.

En Route

Imagine a restaurant by the deep lake,
travelers' loud clatter. Sun in the window,
bright squares. A boy orders fries,
a mother holds a baby who doesn't like being held,
a father opens a menu. Strangers
at the thick wood tables. Ice tea. Hamburgers.
The boy asks about the light, can he climb it?
The mother wipes the baby's face with her fingers,
sets him down on the floor.
The waitress wears blue shorts, a pony tail.
She remembers everything in her head.
It is already the 21st century.
This family is polite and faithful.
Chances are good they will drive home safely.
There are clean diapers and enough milk.
The boy asks again if he can climb the light.
He wants an answer.

II

You can't have it back, says the fire
affectionately. You never needed it
anyway, promises the earth.

— Dean Young

Psalm

A poem should always contain a staff
even if it's bought at the Halloween store.
A poem should remember laughter.
A poem should squeeze sweat
from between its lines
to remind you that words
are muscles – they can punch you
in the gut harder than Heracles.
Heracles should never appear
in a poem because he's already
won plenty of medals.
A poem should pierce your heart gladly
even when the daughter turns
from the mother and keeps walking.
You see the scene clearly,
the tremor at the edge of the lost
girl's mouth, the useless maternal hand.
A poem is water with cucumber,
a hunk of sour dough bread.
A poem leads you away from the one
who died, even while she remains
a few feet distant, unable to speak.
You wish the poem were a cradle.
You wish the poem could sing
away your shame.
A poem contains all things,
but not that.

Thanksgiving Dinner

You were so white, fog-like,
leaning outside the airport for a smoke,
your shirt tucked carefully into your slacks
another size smaller.
All weekend you pretended for our sake,
but the cancer leaked out, rank,
and you slept through those three afternoons –
your body's decay embarrassed you.
Your first born lay on the couch, dazed by depression,
my boys bickered loudly as they played.
I brought out Thanksgiving dinner
with candles and cloth napkins,
colored crystal and gold-rimmed plates.
We leaned into each other for the picture.
Gone by Christmas, you still smile within my grip.

Gathering Asphodel

In the old days you'd be a shade
puttering in the Elysium fields,
looking for a trowel,
your pockets full of seeds,
keeping busy.
You were always up to something –
washing dishes or writing a musical.
Your apparent stillness in the earth
is so unlike you.
If you saw all the little tasks
you'd left undone
and the thousands since you left,
you'd surely return
with a mending kit or glue.
But they threw too much
weight on top,
they packed the dirt in tight,
they didn't know
you never intended to go
in the first place, mistakes were made,
and now you're stuck in that bed
without even a telephone.

For My Mother

In your backyard pool
you breast-stroked slowly across
and back, I sat on the rung,
my feet idle, watching you
circle the bent-in vinyl rim
with complete contentment, *this,*
you said, *is just right,*
your pale arms paddling
there and back, there and back,
like a small ship, a ferry
that had once carried me
and landed us safely here
with calm, unhurried strokes
to this poolside by lush weeds,
a mass of uncut grass, and peach trees.

*   *   *

You were our high horn note, our cheery
print pants in the grocery store,

our sofa cushion
where you read your Agatha Christies
sucking your thumb —

What they say about teen moms is a lousy lie —
you were our tough guide, our armor

against his barbs,
our buoy, our rudder, our humor,

our TV dinner, our bird-feeder, cat-rescuer,
neighbor-suspicious secret-keeper doctor-snubber,
free-thinking, forward-looking fatalist.

You snipped chewing gum from my hair,
left us a little house.

You believed in happiness.

*   *   *

Rain. Real rain
so that I ran out to close
the car windows.

At first the ground
sipped it with a strange
sound, like rubber-soled shoes
skidding on a gym floor.

I had been asleep, almost,
not believing it could rain here
in July
though the sky

had been filling itself all day
like a child carefully coloring
a paper sky with gray clouds,

which is how I now imagine it —

a child gripping a crayon
intent on his work
and then tearing it up.

And then, my mind
goes again to you
in the ground, getting wet.

* * *

Silence afterwards, wave-lengths of words
undulating, inaudibly, in the body

like your death, boxed, buried, but
still concussing inside us, a quiet

mushroom cloud smothered by distance,
as in those photos, the forlorn

fixed on a faraway ridge, flimsy glasses
unable to break the bomb's shock, and so

dumb innocence gives way to grief.
Our cells twitch, reparable, while yours

bloat and burst under the scrubby ground.
Struck, rung, hollowed,

we hear your last words' decay,
traveling those many miles to reach us.

*   *   *

No queendom there,
no husband to blame —

You went willingly, alone,
indifferent to the clothes we chose.

So the story had it wrong —
the mother goes first

into the cramped box
where there is no sweetness

but herself,
where death eats her

slowly
without gratitude or pleasure,

for his task is indiscriminate.
And her daughter remains

here
among the threshed

and fallen grain,
waiting the years.

*   *   *

You said heaven would be
whatever I wanted,
and so I wish the same for you —

You always liked the long view
from the roof of your house
balanced on stilts,
how you could look past palms
across the mazed canals.
You liked to smoke up there,
where the Gulf wind cooled your skin,
which was freckled and soft
like an old cloth doll's.

I wish that for you,
the feeling of safe height,
sight of sluggish water, turtles,
a blue heron aloft.

When you climb down
you will feel refreshed, ready
now to shut the door.

By Now

from your grave
wisps of grass
as sparse as your pale hair.

Down there,
your body is busy
feeding roots.

Isn't that what mothers do?

You cook inside a strange kitchen
in a dark house.

These six years —
as if you'd just stepped away
to turn the oven off.

Ode to Keats

But of course death
blackens breath,
hacks up a bone, conjures
rags, vials, tinctures,

streaked bedsheets, flies.
Not much to do but
lay a cool cloth across the eyes
and listen to that — what? —

nightingale, naturally.
Who wouldn't drowse
when doubt-stricken, aroused
by half-heard melody?

Darkling, you say, to die
sublimed by bird song.
Luscious death wish
steeped in incense.

Darling, your ardent
self yearns me a lot.
Influence or influenza?
Tell me, is earth enough?

Emptying

So cold in Ohio that March day
we emptied out Mom's storage unit.
Naturally, I remember only what we tossed —
the whimsical homemade poster
from her buddies at NCR
bidding her goodbye
when Dad lured her back into his life,
a crocheted throw
folded into a zippered plastic bag
made by my friend's mother
thirty years ago, her spent cigarette
smoke leaking from the bag,
snow floating sideways,
neither of us in gloves, you fretful and angry,
I took the bag and lobbed it
into the off-limits dumpster.
The poster, too. Hard to give up.
Hard to keep. Just the sight of those things
made me sad, yet
to have trashed them . . .
We didn't even finish that day,
did we? The cold was arctic,
swept straight across the plains
through the house where Dad still lived,
wind making that dead sound in the silage,
rushing right through our useless coats.
The cold knew what we were up to,
puny humans emptying a life.
It embraced us. Merciless.

Prescription

— for my brother

Eat a whole mango, its bitter skin
and drippy pulp through to its hairy seed.
Relish the time it takes to pick your teeth
standing on your back porch
watching the dogs run.
By then another hour will have passed.

Feed the dogs. Give Toby her thyroid pill.
Don't assume Robbie is sad.
Don't assume anything.

Plan a trip through the Slavic countries,
the ones with dusky histories and bright,
peppery names. Stay a while in Romania.
Imagine how great grandma Freedman
lived before the papers came.
You've got grandpa's face,
how he could grin through the worst.

How's the mango tasting? Hold a piece
of its leathery skin under your tongue.
Or spit it out. Who cares? I'm not looking.

Did you get dressed this morning? Go to Walmart
and buy the biggest air mattress on the shelf,
hell, buy a pool too with a filter and cover
and gadgets and picture instructions.
It should take at least three days
just to unfold its sleek vinyl walls.

Then you get to watch your dogs jump in.
Nothing's as happy as a happy dog.

We're all coming to visit. I hear your septic tank
is fixed. Show off your coin collection, your rare books.
We won't go till you tell each story.
Snow's falling already?
That's what Ohio's like, you know that by now.
By March the driveway's full of mung
and the sun's got a permanent film as bad as Plexiglas.
Who wouldn't feel crappy peeling plastic wrap
from another instant dinner? Call me.
We'll laugh at the stupid things Dad did.
We'll forgive each other.

Don't go yet. The world's too screwy without you.
Come see these blue dragonflies touch down
on beach grass. Remember you took me up
in that 4-seater plane? And the alarm went off?
Jesus! That's all I have to say about that.
I'm sending a U-Haul to pick up all your dumb
firearms. Get the leash. Robbie and Toby
are licking your shins, ready for a walk.
Take up with a pastry chef.
Become a lepidopterist.

Duty Call

We stopped at the FOP outside Kokomo,
10 pm, no one at the bar, and sat
on cracked vinyl under the muted tube,
tried out a cheery phrase or two
as the bored gal poured us drinks.
You bought a scratch ticket
that paid for my tonic,
said you always got lucky –
but the vodka played tricks on you,
your oily thoughts crept back,
you were ready to turn around,
make the four-hour drive back to Johnstown,
but I said no. Outside, freezing rain,
a father five blocks away
sunk in the smoke-stained couch,
watching COPS.
It's been the same for fifty years,
a hundred, thousands –
the father's need to crush the son,
the son's heart untying its knots.
We zipped our coats, climbed into the car,
and headed over to the old man
who came to the door barefoot,
his lit cigarette in hand.

Goldilocks

The door listed open
into a room that stunk
of porridge prepared by bear.
Each bowl sat on the stone tabletop.
She imagined them grunting, gruel
leaking from their lips.
She touched the rough linens
smeared with scraps.
When she pushed a spoon in,
a cloud dimmed the room
and she remembered her father's
breath as he pinched her neck,
her mother's crusted scalp,
how she wished for a sister
she could put on the mantle
and undress.
Her own clothes felt suddenly thick,
crinoline sheaves of sweat
stuck to her hips,
it was no use sitting
on the splintered Adirondack
slats, it was straight to bed,
but which?
Before the bears found her
she'd need to adjust her limbs
to the cot's cramped mattress
in the swoon
she'd rehearsed back home,

the mirror's mean light reflecting
nothing but the broken
gold of her hair.
She lay on the smallest bed.
She watched the shallow
bulges of her breasts
lift and fall.

Finding Him

All the ashtrays tremble with the overflow
of snuffed cigarettes, glass or clay vessels
with their arrangement of old ash
and crumpled filters — one touch and several
spent inch-long butts topple over the edge
like paper petals on the shag carpet.
Even mugs, lumpy and beloved, fashioned
by grandchildren, are filled with
ashen potpourri. They tip them gingerly
into the plastic trash bag, the last loved items
that felt the father's lips.
His children search out evidence
as they clear the house —
slacks with his belt threaded through,
pockets emptied, sheets wadded up,
the urine-soaked mattress and box spring.
Between couch cushions a syringe,
kids' broken toys, a bloody Kotex,
every kitchen spoon bent level.
The junkies who'd fleeced their father
left a condom under the TV.
We changed the sheets
but there's an odor in the room.
When they found him upstairs,
windows filmy, jammed shut,
the air thick with burning uric acid,
he lay curled on his side,
his arms clutched to his chest,

thin as a boned chicken.
He gripped his face with blackened nails.
What are you doing here?
They peeled the wet blankets back and began
to bring him back to something human.

Last Days

It seemed he'd already decided
to die, steeped in his own urine
in a room dense with acid fumes,
windows wedged shut, curtains
spilling dust. He lay on his side,
the drenched sheet twisted,
a blackened bedsore burnt into his backside.
We tipped him up despite his howling,
figured a way to slide him
onto the other twin bed.
Simply the sheet brushing his toes
startled out agonized cries.
My brother and I were stupid kids again,
knowing nothing when he said
he had to pee and had even managed
to nudge his legs over the edge of the bed,
we said, that's okay, go ahead,
not knowing he was blocked
until the surgeon jammed a needle
into his bladder and shoved
larger and larger catheters to open him.
He would have died,
left at home — what home it was.
I stroked his head as he writhed,
his eyes blanched, imploring me,
but we brought him back
for six weeks, barely able to speak
for the brain tumor and renal failure,

Will you want a feeding tube?
Should we go that route? the doctor
asked in a rather upbeat way,
and I wasn't sure which misery
to choose or which would finally
claim him as he slumped
in the wheelchair, delicately picking
a few M&Ms from my palm.
He could still feed himself
but forgetfully, and once
introduced himself by name.
I sat beside him with a crossword puzzle
and he said *ohm*
was *resistance*, but when I asked
what book followed Genesis
he clawed again at his IV line.
That's when I put the pencil down.

At This Hour

The sun likes to bend through glass —
anything to sharpen itself.

And the grass licks itself
all over, making a silvery sound,

announcing its knives.
At this hour the lupine fades,

crows congregate in their black
outfits, flicking the wormy dirt.

Beyond them — slow oaks, a strip
of bay water, blue

as cataracts. And now
gnats rise from the loam,

traveling on transparent currents,
useless flecks, like sawdust.

Hospital Museum

They chose lights too dim to read by
and cheap bedside stands.
This one has a drawerful of M&Ms.

A table displays a vase of brown-tipped carnations,
a stack of opened cards.
Each room offers a view of sky,
a TV screen bolted to the wall.

They have endeavored to preserve
the cold tubular beds, waffle-weave blankets,
the plastic privacy curtain,
a rolling IV pole.

The patient's imprint is still there
in obvious declivities,
a Dixie cup on its ring of sweat.

Even so, despite the bright brochures,
visitors flinch from the familiar antiseptic.
Everyone who goes knows what's gone.

III

Thou, silent form, dost tease us out of thought
As doth eternity: Cold Pastoral!
                                    — John Keats

Postcard

Now I'm the one absent.
No redwoods in sight.
No ocean fog-stippling-light
en route to school. Instead,

we're sling-chaired here,
overlooking a vast Mayan-
mown lawn, white oak,
Chinese elm, and long

skeins of honeysuckle
off leash, running over hedges,
raveling – ravishing? – trim privets.
Though no nightingale

regales us, such lush scents
leave us panting. And as if
for nature's hell-of-it,
these nights, already insect-dense,

release firefly confetti.
Boys, here's summer as it's meant:
grass, wasps, thunder, sweat.
Wish you were with me.

Cold Pastoral

Iceland is the world's
youngest country, as in
land discerned by water,
one of those facts that
dost tease us out of thought,
even though thinking is the
one thing we can't not do,
the brain vibrating
in a vast gray fatty matter
insulating ideas
like phreatic eruption
latitudinal biodiversity gradient
karyokinesis
Bremsstrahlung
and Burger King's whopper.
But here in Iceland
fretful clouds shred themselves,
wind brisks the birches,
puffins perch
on volcanic perforations
where the island spewed
and cooled.
What dread umbilicus!
ash and basalt strewn
across tundra,
everywhere a mess.
This baby's been stripped
and left on its own

exposed plateau. Try saying
Hvannadalshnukur, a place only
indulgent aunts will visit.
Easy enough now
to find on the map —
but just ask about
95% of the universe,
and no one knows where it is.

Dear Odysseus

What else to do these desperate
days since your departure
but find use for earth's lively detritus?
After his long entreaties
I let the local embalmer practice
his hobby on me: drenching
the skin of middle-aged women
with honeydew. Luckily
six kids on skateboards
brought drops from the shiny
tips of jewel-weed to rinse
my Russian eyes.
My neighbor the blonde
New York astrologer
painted my lips with a paste
of *funghi divini*
that grow only in the dusty
playgrounds of the Bronx.
She promises its musk
will rouse you even
in the fleshless shudders of eternity.
Next I rubbed mint leaves
behind my knees
to prolong the pungent minutes
en route to the inner thigh
where I've prepared a surprise.
And from a horse I've plucked
three strands of mane

to braid into a loose leash
you may use as you wish.
Just this morning
in the damp hour before dawn
I chewed the fragrant *Poeticus Narcissus*
with whose petals
I've scented this page.

Vagabond

Even now I know little
about you, though you've left plenty
of prints on me, my skin
a damp terrain of vanishing
impressions, while
you jump ship, skip bail,
ride the rails back east.
I've been trailing you
my whole life,
carrying my cardboard cup
of tepid coffee and a suitcase
stuffed with childhood letters
too brittle to open anymore.
I find my platform
packed with cheerleaders –
bunches of beribboned
excitable lilies –
and two widows eyeing their pink
pompoms approvingly.
When the locomotive lurches in
my brain feels emptied
flushed and shamed all at once.
Steam jets from between iron
wheel spokes in spurts.
I'm bathed in a burnt
cindery perfume.
Someone lifts my suitcase
through a darkened door.

There's the usual tearful
goodbyes, crumpled
sandwich wrappers,
brisk kisses. Those pompoms
press at the windows
like babies' faces.
It seems my ticket's tucked
in a forgotten pocket.
I'm hoping some stranger —
maybe that mild man
sweeping the sidewalk —
will tell me if I'm to embark
or whether I've just
arrived.

Eros

Imagine his hairy, plush arms,
imagine being lifted,
your breasts gently rocking

as he walks across the corn
fields you'd always loved,
across the little stream

you'd sipped clean water from
as a child, kneeling
in cool mud,

and now he carries you
as high as the hill
that makes this valley,

blue-gray flame
against a paler sky,
the very place your eye

would rest on
like a caress,
where now you reach

around his neck
as he turns his back
on all that,

preparing to take you
over the horizon
that rises like something cut

from construction paper,
uneven greens and browns
wrapped around your life,

opening now,
the life you'd loved,
the life you are leaving

for this.

Imaginary Lover

What's his connection with you, oh playful stranger
With whom I have danced drunkenly,
Thinking, "The more I dance, the more I want to"
                — Alicia Ostriker

Oh imaginary, oh actual,
though the fly buzzes brazenly
and the steady thrum of bulldozers
drums the hills,
though duty and love keep our gaze fixed
to the "true north,"

oh, the strings still unfurl like tongues,
like dancing kites or tightropes
across which costumed flirtations
wheel back and forth, grazing

the playful urging of our eyes.
Distance is, of course, necessary,
as with any art.
What I know of the Kama-Sutra
is simply this: *prolong, prolong.* And so
I allow myself to imagine us

as mutual, partners in a polka
whirling among the guests,
or else secret, asleep in a boat, the lake
like a large animal dozing in the sun
whose slow breath rocks us,
pillowed on each other's damp arms

from which we refuse to awaken,
preferring the dream of endless arousal,
endless repose. Desire plays in the mind
like a strand of old music
from a tinny radio, the one
you turned up whenever the right song came on,

back when all lovers were lush inventions,
shapely designs to please the soul
whose appetite, it seemed, would last
for as long as these pop songs
drifting along the shore.

Looking Ahead

Energy may take various forms...
but there is never any net gain or net loss...
— Samuel A. Marantz

If such could be: energy
never lost, let me

be the cool drop
your tongue finds

at midday
digging weeds

from our poor
hillside garden.

I'd hide
as a doorstop or

bottle cap,
crescent of soap

sudsing
your shaving dish.

Better yet, I'd feel
both your hands

holding me as you roll
out biscuit dough.

Let some strand
of my hair

latch on
to your ear,

or find me
nested

in the soft pocket
of your pants.

I may be the mouse
you curse,

strewing crackers
behind the stove,

an Alpine cloud
shadowing your view,

an ice cube
watering your drink.

I may be the last
pinch of salt

in your aunt's
glass cellar,

enough to savor
your beef stew.

And if you should
likewise be

rearranged,
no longer cinched

by these familiar cells,
let us rove

as beetles by the pond
(you know the one)

our antennae touching lightly
as we pass.

Ars Poetica

Why do words, when chimed, make you weep?

Dean's "dream in the daylit / consciousness,"
for instance.

Birds are so lucky, they sing warning, threat,
important stuff,
while we butcher the slightest things.

You can spend hours counting syllables,
practicing an advanced syntax – still

Merrill's thoughts strewn over strict lines
like a river knocked around by rocks
knock you out.

Same as rescue: the children all grown up
after years kept in a basement.
Refugees rebuilding burned-out homes.

Of beauty Keats says: "truth."
Stevens: "death."

We live in simplified times.

Finding rhyme's easy enough. Sometimes
what's needed is a stone
stumbling your stride.

It's summer here, plenty of gravel.

A cloud-suffused sky
manages its blossoms,
a bunch of white fractals in a blue bowl.

Cumulonimbus so slow and soft up there

pushing airplanes around,
spilling your drink, but not
casting you down,

just casting shadows here on earth

where what keeps us stuck to the ground
even Einstein guessed at.

The best questions go unanswered
though we ask and ask, like Michael Moore
on the bottom floor of the Sears tower.

The big cheese upstairs has fish to fry,
a rainbow trout with caper sauce and butter
browned off the backs of NAFTA mechanics.

But if rhyme's too easy, more so single targets:
politicos in place, contracts signed,
a country's history pops Roger out.

And so...
(a deft ellipsis brings me back)

to gravity, my theme.
Or beauty? Both, like train cars
coupling, pinky finger-linked for miles.

Pain and joy —
even atoms want their mates.
Though also unpredictable:

nerves, like lightning, have their own agendas.

When there's much to say you close the door.

You type it up then write back into it.

What you're looking for —
a canteen flung in road dust,
a neighbor with a crowbar
splintering the door —

you can't help but swear

somewhere, between the lines, it's there.

In the Next Life

You'll slip into the ocean's
inky dungeons, reborn
as a two-ton squid,
or reappear as that same
mosquito you squashed
while hiking through
New Jersey's pine barrens.
You'll feel your soul squeeze
into Rush Limbaugh's manic
descendant, a baseball cap
distributor for the northeast coast,
a man who fled home
only to find himself pawning
the slim silver necklace
his grandmother had given him.
You might be snow packed
into a girl's acrylic mitten
or a taste bud
as she licks the snow.
You may wince while clipped
from the dictator's moustache
or shine in the small
jar of polish his wife likes.
If asked, I'd choose something
simple, more mute
than my present incarnation,
to return as a wild strip
of loosestrife I glimpsed once

while riding up front in a truck,
or else a June bug
stuck to a screen, mating.
I'd like to try being
a breeze that touches the hot
cheeks of a bawling infant,
to enter her lungs
and cool the cramped
muscle of her heart.
Think of it – someday
your flesh will feed
stinkbug and jewel weed.
May your spirit tumble
in the moist tower
of a troublesome
thundershower.

Ode to That

When duty calls, you are demonstrative...

double-jointed knuckle,
swinging bridge,
quick bucket brigade
between phrases,
you serve your subjects
with dignity,
carrying messages
under a brimmed hat
without ever reading
them yourself.
Lovers' humble go-between,
empty of fact
yet pregnant with intent,
a handshake
between strangers,
a traveler's delicate
sandal print refusing rest,
you make sure things
receive their essence,
whether they be
the queen's royal foot
(lovely of length,
regrettably stinky)
or the pig's archaic grunt —
O relative pronoun!
O verbal glue!
so few applaud
your honest work

without which
(forgive me my use of
your upstart kin)
we'd lack
such lush restriction . . .

> *The pollen that sought*
> *his own kind*
> *flew from stigma to stigma*
> *to sweet sticky stigma*
> *finally bursting*
> *deliciously*
> *inside the narrow-throated*
> *camas lily.*

All That You See

All that you see, even the vast
incomprehensible sky,
will pass.

Dark matter, dark energy —
whatever the real is —
there will be collisions

without scars
or flesh to feel them.

Apocalypse?

The Bible predicts,
the science is secure.
It's set down in words

vetted by experts,
pronounced by God.

Revelation?

Perhaps a flash
of something small,
possibly given.

Blue

Blue rivers in the wrist,
the Pacific's enormous pulse,
a boy's lips shivering.

Blue jeans open at the crotch
draped on a fence.
Blue hydrangeas, cornflowers, delphiniums.

Cobalt straight from the tube
to blue-shadowed thighs.

A dying father's eyes
washed of all but blue,
bereft at last.

A bride's blue handkerchief
gripped for remembrance.

Blue milk. Blue moon.
Code blue in the trauma unit.
Blue pieces of fetus.

Blue ink leveled by lined paper.
Words secured against
the inevitable sky.

Anthology: a collection of flowers

You thought bees' wings made that hum
but the buzzing is breath,
the body lined with vibrating flutes.
That's the kind of information I love:
photosynthesis in asparagus, sperm
that can smell lilies of the valley,
how to solve for the hypotenuse, I love that,
you should have heard the roofers laugh
as they sawed into the rafters.
Maybe it's best not to care
whether they understand the comma.
Like big deep heavy shovelfuls of snow
is grading papers, scraping
along the sidewalk you know
is buried there, somewhere,
a firm argument under the fluff.
Aren't thirty years enough? Forty?
Surely all they'll remember is Laila
putting me in a grass skirt
to teach me hula. Use a paper bag
until it softens and the seams
give out, getting old's like that.
Weird to think your ancient teachers
are still around, even now!
Mr. Kotary! He was just a kid
teaching trig in that disastrous school,
throwing erasers at us.
That was back when teachers broke
blackboards to get our attention.

Now humiliation does the trick —
rationing bathroom passes.
What is it they want to teach?
What is it we want to know?
The PhD told me after the last surgery
he woke up having forgotten everything:
dimensions, formulae, how to paint in the lines.
Goodbye tenured appointment. Hello
world-class wine-making. Some losses
are like that. Terminal velocity
softens the fall. The cat can drop
thirty-two stories and skitter away.
Can the same be said of a cow?
When the candidate comes to campus
what are we looking for?
Questions circle the room
close to the floor. We conclude
whoever invented the desk chair
should be hog-tied to one,
a sort of medieval punishment.
That's another thing I love, Middle English
like a foundling wrapped in wet nappies
it took a whole country to keep alive
just by talking. Chaucer,
you had me at "Whan that Aprille,"
I'd have leapt into bed with you,
even a lousy bed. Despite the years,
underneath our strange apparel
we look much the same.
My students are too polite to point,
I never know what they're feeling.
Are they feeling? Ruth Stone remembers

the old curtains in the place
where her husband hung himself.
It's not a test. Maybe words
have leaked gas and the poem won't start.
Maybe it's me, closer to the end
than to birth, dreaming of death.
Harold, I'd like you to draw me
big again, next to the vanishing tracks.

Moon

We didn't have to have one –
just serendipity and luck, a chunk
flung into orbit, and there

you are, gleaming and pretty,
our white gem –
yes, cold, the scientists tell us,

and distant, though the eye
embraces you as easily as
an apple in a bowl –

a whole apple tonight,
tomorrow, a slice.

Notes

"Dear Future" — the epigraph comes from Dave Praeger's *Poop Culture: How America is Shaped by its Grossest Natural Product*.

"Global Weirding" — I owe this expression to naturalist David Lucas.

"Ode to QI" celebrates the comedic British quiz show hosted until 2015 by Stephen Fry along with his sidekick Alan Davies. The line, "Poetry is a good provider of the strange," is lifted from Dean Young's poem "Non-Apologia."

"Looking Ahead" — the epigraph comes from my high schoolphysics book, *Brief Review in Physics*, by Samuel A.Marantz.

"Anthology: a collection of flowers" — much of the information comes from the quiz show QI.

Acknowledgments

Many thanks to the magazines and anthologies in which the following poems appeared:

Canary: "Dear future"
Cider Press Review: "Grass Seeds," "Remember These Things," "Imaginary Lover"
Forklift, OH: "Cold Pastoral"
JAMA: "Hospital Museum"
The Gettysburg Review: "Ode to That"
The Healing Art of Writing: "Prescription"
The Hollins Critic: "Psalm"
Homestead Review: "Looking Ahead"
Marin Poetry Center Anthology: "Moon"
Poetry East: "Gathering Asphodel"
Spillway: "En Route," "All That You See," "Dear Odysseus," "Vagabond"
The Squaw Review: "Pet Cat," "Sudden Rain" (in "For My Mother" sequence)
Tell Me Again: "By Now"
Tor House.org: "Believing"
Tuxedo Literary Magazine: "Big History"
Blackbird: "From This Distance" and "Anthology: a collection of flowers"

I'm deeply grateful to the Community of Writers at Squaw Valley and the Virginia Center for the Creative Arts, where many of these poems were written, and to Dominican University of California for providing sabbatical support, to David St John and the Cloud View Poets for their candid and warmhearted critiques,

to my fellow Ensenada Avenue poets—Judy Halebsky, Dawn McGuire, Claudia Mon Pere, Ann Pelletier, and Barbara Tomash—for their astute editorial guidance and friendship,

to my mentor Alicia Ostriker for her invaluable help when I thought I was "done,"

to John Peterson for his generous acceptance of this book just at the right time.

Author Biography

Joan Baranow is the author of *Living Apart* and two poetry chapbooks. Her poems have appeared in *The Paris Review, The Gettysburg Review, Spillway*, and elsewhere. A VCCA fellow and member of the Community of Writers at Squaw Valley, she founded and directs the Low-Residency MFA program in Creative Writing at Dominican University of California. With her husband David Watts, she produced the PBS documentary *Healing Words: Poetry & Medicine*. Her feature-length documentary, *The Time We Have*, presents an intimate portrait of a young woman facing terminal illness.

CPSIA information can be obtained
at www.ICGtesting.com
Printed in the USA
BVHW031119280219
541429BV00002B/363/P